Cooperative Learning, Thinking and Problem Solving

Grades 2 through 4

by
James Sonnenberg
Allan Windsor

Illustrated
by
Lynda Lawson

Publishers
T.S. Denison & Company, Inc.
Minneapolis, Minnesota 55431

A special thanks to Julie Bolinger for her assistance.
Thanks also, to Alice Zimmer and Theresa Bauer for
their encouragement and support.

Standard Book Number: 513-02059-4
Cooperative Learning, Thinking and Problem Solving
Copyright © 1991 by the T.S. Denison & Co., Inc.
Minneapolis, MN 55431

Forward for Teachers

This book is designed to help teachers implement technology concepts, problem solving skills, and social interaction techniques in grades two, three and four.

After the first lesson, open the book to any project, they are not arranged in sequential order. Once a choice is made you can begin sparking students' interest by referring to the project throughout the week.

Table of Contents

Cooperative Projects

The Magic 25:
Helpful hints to get you going

1. Once begun, most projects need very little teacher direction.

2. You will be helping children learn the mechanics of learning, therefore, allow students to experiment.

3. Be innovative, creative. The directions are not cut in stone.

4. Only one or two of the projects require students to follow specific teacher directions.

5. All projects are accomplished within **cooperative learning groups** of approximately six students.

6. Group cohesion is a major objective.

7. These groups do not have to be static. I call each cooperative learning group a "factory."

8. Technologically speaking, if something does not work, you change it until it does. You as the teacher can direct this competitiveness in a positive direction.

9. Most projects will require at least an hour. Always give them a 10 minute warning before it is finishing time.

10. Each factory is responsible for total operation, from distribution of materials to clean-up.

11. Factories may need to vote for a supervisor, supply distributor, quality control personnel, and workers. (Supervision at this point will ensure each student the opportunity to participate at different levels.)

12. All materials are dispensed from a central location. Each supply personnel will collect necessary materials.

13. You may want a couple of large boxes for material storage. Many of the items are reusable.

14. Other than the first *lesson* projects are not in sequential order.

15. Most projects require factories to cooperatively complete one project.

16. Products are displayed and each factory's personnel votes who can take the finished product home.

17. Criteria for the weekly project can be listed on the chalkboard.

18. If informed throughout the week, students may bring some of the materials from home. Thus, you are sparking their interest even before the project has begun.

19. If you do not want to pay out of your own pocket for some of the items, work them into your yearly budget.

20. The edible projects, for twenty-six students, averages around five/six dollars.

21. If your school has an account at a local store, use it!

22. Some food items for the edible projects may be acquired from your school lunch program.

23. Some projects require cutting instruments, teacher's discretion is advised.

24. Use your school kitchen for borrowing pots, pans, dishes, utensils, etc. Use the teacher's lounge microwave.

25. Calculation of expenses by students may sometimes be required. This can be one of your criteria. A penny, nickel, or a dime per item can be calculated by each factory in coming up with total cost.

PROJECT SUMMARY CHART

PROJECT	DATE USED	COMMENTS
#1 Popcorn Day		
#2 Bridge Building		
#3 Matters of Importance		
#4 Short Tall Tales		
#5 Stack the Deck		
#6 Moving a Milk Carton		
#7 Tower Power		
#8 Medical Complex		
#9 Pumpkin Heads		
#10 Our Teacher's Report Card		
#11 Nursery Rhymes/Synonyms		
#12 Technology Collage		
#13 Hare and Tortoise Race		
#14 Pea and Toothpick Building		
#15 Paper Airplane Building		
#16 Pinwheels		
#17 A Polaroid Polarity		
#18 Graham Cracker Decorating		
#19 Build It – Move It		
#20 Make Me a Rainbow		
#21 45 Minutes to 4		
#22 The Paper Plate Dilemma		
#23 Marshmallow Olympics		
#24 A Newspaper Activity		
#25 Food Groups Collage		
#26 Spelling With Our Fingers		
#27 Desesrt Survival		

T.S. Denison & Co., Inc.

Cooperative Learning,
Thinking and Problem Solving

POPCORN DAY

RATIONALE:

This introductory lesson will acquaint the student with the concept of cooperative learning groups. This lesson will also lay out the format for the following week's technology activities. Remember, you will be helping children learn the mechanics of learning, therefore, allow students to experiment.

OBJECTIVE:

The students, in their cooperative learning groups, will devise a method of equally distributing popcorn and a beverage for their snack.

MATERIALS:

1 bag of microwave popcorn (popped) for each group. Two 2 liter containers of pop or 1 gallon of koolaid. A small bowl, a glass, and a napkin for each student. (If informed throughout the week, students may bring some of the materials from home.) Thus, you are sparking their interest even before the project has begun.

PROCEDURE:

1. Have students arrange desks for a group activity. These groups do not have to be static. You, as the teacher, may have already selected the members of each group.

2. Brainstorm! Discuss and list what personnel may be required for today's project. They should also discuss the materials and supplies they may need. Factories may need to vote for a boss/supervisor, and inspector, a display person, supply personnel, distributor, quality control personnel, and line assembly workers. (Supervision at this point will allow each student the opportunity to participate at different levels.)

3. The supply personnel will come to the central dispersal area (the teacher's desk) to obtain the supplies for their group.

In this activity they will need one popped bag of corn (remember the teacher's lounge microwave). If a beverage is provided, each will need a small glass too. Keeping the beverage at the central dispersal area can be a cooperative sharing experience in itself. You may also have each factory designate one from their group, to work as a separate group, to make the koolaid.

4. The objective is for each group to equally distribute popcorn and beverage, for each individual in the group, in as cooperatively a manner as possible. The criteria to be followed here may be that the finished product is put on "display" and viewed by all before each group is allowed to indulge.

FOLLOW-UP:

A few minutes spent in discussion with each group, prior to clean-up, can make everyone aware of some of the problems that were encountered. What was successfully done or not done within each group to deal with these problems can also be shared. Remember Teacher, once they have started, stay out of it as much as possible. Observe and record positives and negatives for later discussion. The teacher's responsibility is to highlight and evaluate situations for the benefit of each student.

BRIDGE BUILDING

RATIONALE:
Students working in groups will construct a bridge.

OBJECTIVE:
Within a 40 minute time period and working in cooperative learning groups, students will construct a suspension bridge with supplied materials. The bridge must be at least 12 inches long and support a designated classroom dictionary.

MATERIALS:
Each group will be supplied with 1 roll of masking tape, 10 large straws, 12 small straws, 10 rubber bands, 20 paper clips, 2 milk cartons (from their milk break), 1 ruler and one pencil. They will also need a blank sheet of paper. The groups can decide what they will and won't use.

PROCEDURE:
1. Students can assemble into their cooperative learning groups. They can arrange the room.

2. They will elect the needed personnel. They will need a supervisor, engineers, supplier, workers and an accountant.

3. The criteria are explained. You may want to web the word "suspension."

    a. They will build a suspension bridge at least 12 inches long.

    b. The bridge, when placed between two chairs, must be able to hold a designated book.

    c. They will also compute the cost of building the bridge. For this they will need a calculator.

    Each piece of tape = 1¢
    Each straw = 1¢
    Each rubber band = 1¢
    Each paper clip = 2¢

d. They will be given 35 minutes.

4. Materials are dispensed and the time limit begins.

FOLLOW-UP:

This project has allowed the group to cooperate; some interesting construction should have taken place.

Now is the time of reckoning. Each group is to test their bridge. They may also want to add more books to see just how much the bridge will hold.

After each group has demonstrated their creations, discussion can take place. Again, discuss problems encountered and solutions selected. Praise, appraise, compare, contrast and support their ambitions. At this time allow the accountants to report on the total cost of their group's project.

Bridges can be displayed, collapsed or not, and the room is brought back to order.

MATTERS OF IMPORTANCE

(Resource materials are needed)

RATIONALE:
Students learn about relevant scientific concepts.

OBJECTIVE:
Each cooperative learning group will decide on and select their project subject. Then, using the available selected resources, write a report.

Note: Depending on the grade level, the report can be vocabulary awareness and definition in a written report with the construction of visual aids to be used in a display. The reports may also be taped and used as a student authored library resource.

MATERIALS:
Use the concepts and vocabulary list included here or decide upon some of your own. Each group will also need resource materials (your librarian or an aid can be helpful now). Each group will also need pencils and some paper.

PROCEDURE:
1. The cooperative learning groups will assemble at their work areas.

2. Allow each group to choose or you devise a method of distributing a concept title to each group. Along with the title, provide a list of the relevant vocabulary.

3. The groups may select researchers and recorders. There are enough vocabulary words and there should be enough resource materials available so each member can fulfill a role.

4. Have the resource materials displayed (this may be done days prior to the project). Now each group may decide and select what they think they can use. Be sure the selection is thorough enough so they do not have to waste time searching.

Cooperative Learning,
Thinking and Problem Solving

5. Time allotment for this project will depend on the grade level and the depth of research required. Forty-five minutes to one hour should be sufficient.

FOLLOW-UP:
Praise, appraise and support their efforts. Each group may now report on their findings. An additional project or class period may involve groups in the construction of visual aids to enhance their report.

Relevant scientific concepts:

<u>Common Predators</u>

preying mantis
snake
red fox
skunk
raccoon
American toad
black widow spider
golden eagle

<u>Endangered Species</u>

jaguars
gray wolves
peregrine falcons
cougars
bald eagle
grizzly bear
sea otter
American alligator

<u>Pollution</u>

acid rain
rain forest
weather
ozone
emissions
solar energy
carpool
pesticide

<u>Our Environment</u>

desert
wetland
woodland
river
habitat
soil/soil conservation
fresh water
erosion

SHORT TALL TALES

(Resource materials are needed)

RATIONALE:
Students learn about legendary folk heroes.

OBJECTIVE:
Provided with the name of a folk hero, cooperative learning groups will research and record specific information about the hero and then give a report.

MATERIALS:
Provide a list of American folk heroes. Some you may use are: Paul Bunyon, Davy Crockett, Pecos Bill, Johnny Appleseed, John Henry, Mike Fink, Jonathan Slick, Wind Wagon Smith, Febold Feboldson. Resource materials are provided (the librarian can be very helpful here). One good, older resource book is the 1944 edition of *Tall Tale America*, by Walter Blair, Dewey Decimal 398.2 B. Paper and pencil will also be needed.

PROCEDURE:
1. The cooperative learning groups will gather at their work areas.

2. For this project they will select a recorder and the remaining members form a research team.

3. Distribute paper and pencils.

4. The method of their subject selection may be left up to you.

5. Display ample amounts of resource materials. There is a good variety at all grade levels.

6. Explain that their findings and report must meet the criteria. You may, at your own discretion, require additional information (this, of course, depends on the grade level of the students).

   a. The character (appearance, locale, friends, pets)

   b. Chief exploits/accomplishments

   c. Some amusing incident

7. Thirty to forty minutes should be ample time for the groups to work and be successful.

FOLLOW-UP:
Each group will report their research findings. Discuss problems they encountered and solutions taken. Praise, appraise and support their ambitions. Display each report. Depending on the maturity, each group may also add illustrations.

EXTENSION:
Use these famous people as project subjects: Clara Barton, Sir Walter Raleigh, Betsy Ross, Thomas Edison, Joseph Lister, Booker T. Washington, Helen Keller, Florence Nightingale, or subjects relevant to your specific grade level.

Criteria:

   a. Famous person (name, gender, race, locale, position)

   b. Major accomplishment(s)

   c. Life span (age, dates, age at height of accomplishment)

STACK THE DECK

(A calculator and a deck of playing cards, or 50
math flashcards, are needed for each group.)

RATIONALE:
A "card" tower is constructed as a math project.

OBJECTIVE:
Supplied with a deck of playing cards, or 50 math flashcards, each cooperative learning group will construct a tiered tower and receive points for each card used.

MATERIALS:
One deck of playing cards (well-worn works best) for each group. Fifty math flashcards per group will work too. A calculator, paper and pencil are needed. A small terrycloth towel or a soft cotton towel for each group (to build the tower on). A prize for each group .

PROCEDURE:
1. Students will assemble into their cooperative learning groups.

2. For this project, they will elect a mathematician, a recorder, a supply person, and the rest are construction engineers.

3. Each supply person will select a calculator, the cards, paper and pencil, and a towel for their group.

4. Criteria is displayed and discussed.

   a. Each group begins with 16 cards from which they build the base of their tower (cards will stand when leaned against each other).

   b. Each "base" card is worth 5 points (the group may add or multiply the points by the numbers of cards used, this depends on the grade level).

   c. Now, groups add as many tiers as they can with their remaining cards. **Each card** in tier two is worth 10 points, tier three cards are worth 20 points, etc.

d. Each groups' mathematician and recorder will calculate and record their points.

e. If a group needs more cards, they may negotiate and buy cards from another group. They will pay 5 points per card to whichever group they are able to purchase cards from.

f. They will be given 30 minutes to complete the project.

FOLLOW-UP:
Engineering successes are displayed where built, naturally. Praise their thinking, manipulation and the results of their efforts. Their calculation of points is discussed. Awards/prizes are presented to all.

MOVING A MILK CARTON

RATIONALE:

The cooperative learning groups will use thinking skills to devise a method that will allow them to move a 1/2 pint milk carton.

OBJECTIVE:

Each group, of 5-6 students, working together, will devise two ways to move the carton across the flat surface of their desks. They will not be allowed to touch a carton once it is in motion.

MATERIALS:

Each cooperative learning group will be supplied, from a central location, two one-half pint paper milk cartons (from their milk break or lunch), 24 round toothpicks, two three-foot pieces of string. These two sets of materials can be combined in any manner. Not all of the materials need to be used.

PROCEDURE:

1. Arrangement of desks into a cluster or using a table for each group is recommended.

2. Each group will elect a supervisor. Each group will also elect a supply person. The supervisor supervises and tries to maintain order (Teacher, stay out of it, this can be a learning experience in itself). The supply person will be responsible for gathering the supplies that have been listed on the board. The method of selecting these key figures is left up to each group.

3. Each group may decide to work together to devise the two methods. Or, each group may choose to break into two small groups with each then contributing a method to move the carton; a time limit of 30-35 minutes is sufficient. Time to complete the project, from start to finish, takes approximately one hour.

4. The objective is to discover and demonstrate two different methods of propelling the milk carton across a desk or table top. They may even discover to roll it into a tight ball and bowl it across.

FOLLOW-UP:
At the end of the time limit of cooperative thinking each group will demonstrate their creations to the other groups. After groups have demonstrated their techniques, discussion can take place. This whole class discussion can reveal problems encountered and positive solutions taken to deal with the problems. Problems may result from the group dynamics or from the thinking, manipulation, or operation of the materials. Appraise, compare, contrast, and support their ambitions.

TOWER POWER

RATIONALE:
The students, working in cooperative learning groups of 5 or 6, will construct a tower.

OBJECTIVE:
Within a time period of 30 minutes, using specified materials, the students will construct a free standing tower at least 7 inches tall, that will support an object.

MATERIALS:
These materials may be listed on the board or overhead. The materials will be available and dispensed from a central location. 1 small milk carton for each group (from their milk break). 4 straws. 1 roll of masking tape and 1 large rubber band for each group. 1 large marble or small ball (to be supported by the tower) and a ruler.

PROCEDURE:
1. After the groups are established, and their work space defined, the discussion and procedure can begin as to what personnel will be needed for each group.

2. They should decide, from prior knowledge, that they will need only a manager and a supply person. Once this has been done, then the time limit can begin and they can get their materials and start. They do not have to use all of the specified materials.

FOLLOW-UP:
This project has allowed the groups to cooperate, and some very innovative construction should have taken place. Oh yes, there will be a few remarks about one group taking another group's idea. All of this can be discussed after the time limit is over.

After the time limit:

1. Let each group "show off" their model.

2. Determine if each group has been successful.

3. Discuss problems they encountered and solutions they used. This is one time when your guidance may be appropriate.

4. Appraise, compare, contrast, and support their ambitions.

5. Models and explanations may be put on display for the school to view.

MEDICAL COMPLEX

RATIONALE:

This is a team thinking skill. Students will learn to think together to solve a problem.

OBJECTIVE:

Using a thumb tack and a wooden matchstick the students will, within a 20 minute time limit, determine that they have a pulse and show where it is.

Opening discussion – rely on their prior knowledge. What are some ways for me to tell if someone is alive? Concentrate on the word "pulse." Most students have had their pulse taken at one time or another. At this time **do not** discuss the locations used to find a pulse.

PROCEDURE:

1. They can assemble into their cooperative learning groups of 5-6 students. Each grouping is a "Medical Complex." They are all "Medical Scientists." They are to engage in an experiment.

2. Distribute to each student one thumb tack and a dead wooden matchstick. Tell them that these two objects can be used on themselves to show themselves and others that they have a pulse somewhere.

3. Begin the 20 minute time limit. Be prepared for some bewildered youngsters. Have patience!

4. After 7 to 10 minutes of their free experimentation, open up the groups to free discussion.

   a. Determine if anyone has found where their pulse is.

   b. Ask them, "How could we use the materials we have to aid us to see the pulse?"

   c. This is the time to assist them to assemble their objects.

- The tack is stuck into the center of the unburned end of the matchstick.

- When this is accomplished, the match will sit upright with the tack as its base. A **flat headed** thumb tack works best.

5. Allow them 5-7 minutes to free experiment again. Tell them they are to use the tack and match in an upright position someplace on their body. Discuss where this location may be.

6. Direct them to place the object on their wrist. Tell them to place the object on the underside of their up-turned wrist in line with their pointer finger. Once they are able to hold their arm still and have placed the object correctly they will be able to see it move as a pendulum. They can move the match around anywhere on their wrist. They may also run in place for 20-30 seconds and observe how this affects the movement of the match and tack.

FOLLOW-UP:

Collect the materials. Praise their thinking, manipulation, and the results of their efforts. The room can now be brought back to order.

PUMPKIN HEADS

RATIONALE:

The students, working in cooperative learning groups, will make a decoration.

OBJECTIVE:

Provided with a painted pumpkin, and an assortment of materials, students will work cooperatively as a team, and decorate a pumpkin.

MATERIALS:

1 large pumpkin for each group. A few days before the project, obtain an assortment of bright colored spray paint; give each pumpkin a few good coatings of paint. Red, yellow, blue, black, and green are great colors to use. The morning of the project you may take them into the room in large, closed paper bags. Then just before the project, each group can vote on which bag they would like. It's always a surprise when they open the bags and discover the colored pumpkin they have chosen.

In a central supply area have an assortment of materials to decorate their pumpkins. You may use old wigs, jewelry, paper, felt, and buttons can be used for eyes, nose, and ears. At Halloween time there are numerous face decorating kits available. Use yarn, magazines, etc. Tacks, straight pins, and small nails work well to hold things. Glue *does not* work well.

PROCEDURE:

1. Have the students arrange their work areas, and get into their groups.

2. This is one activity where the group will need only a supply person, except for the workers. They always are needed! The supply person may bring the whole group to the supply table so they may help select what they would like to work with. The order in which groups come up for their supplies is left up to you. You may use a point system based on achievements of the groups during the week prior to this activity. The group earning the most points can be first in selecting which bag they want. You may also draw numbers from a hat.

3. Each group may begin when they have their materials. About 30-40 minutes is ample time for them to work.

FOLLOW-UP:

Have a place cleared where they can set their creations for all to see and enjoy. A discussion may follow as to how things went and how they decided to decorate as they did. Remember in an activity such as this, problems may result from the group dynamics or from the thinking, manipulation, or operation of the materials. Appraise, praise, compare, contrast, and support their ambitions.

Clean up the work area.

Invite other classes in to view the creations.

Be careful! The pumpkins spoil easily in a few days.

OUR TEACHER'S REPORT CARD

RATIONALE:

The students will evaluate their teacher.

OBJECTIVE:

Each cooperative learning group will use the evaluation worksheet and together, answer the evaluation questions.

MATERIALS:

One report card will be given to each cooperative group. Each group will also need a pencil. It may be advantageous for each student to have a copy of the evaluation. (Only one report card per group will be filled out though.)

PROCEDURE:

1. Students will assemble into their cooperative groups.

2. They will select one person to be the recorder and one person to be the reader. The reader may read each statement and then the recorder can mark each answer the group has chosen. Each group may decide to take turns reading the statements.

3. This is the democratic process at work, so remember, there may be some debate.

4. I would suggest that this lesson be used mid-year. Take note of what answers are decided upon by the groups on the reports. They may be somewhat revealing!

FOLLOW-UP:

Collect the evaluations. Assure the students you will go over them carefully. At a later date you may wish to post one report card, with the averaged consensus, somewhere near your desk. Discuss any problems encountered and solutions taken. Thank them for their efforts and honesty.

OUR TEACHER'S REPORT CARD

(Circle your answer)

yes no   1. Our teacher tells us when he/she is pleased with our work.

yes no   2. Our teacher gives us work that is too hard.

yes no   3. Our teacher is interested in things that we do outside of school.

yes no   4. Our teacher listens to what we have to say.

yes no   5. Our teacher gives us work that is too easy.

yes no   6. Our teacher tries to make school interesting for us.

yes no   7. Our teacher does not care about us.

yes no   8. Our teacher treats everyone fair.

yes no   9. Our teacher gives us enough time to finish our work.

yes no   10. Our teacher does not understand us.

yes no   11. Our teacher makes sure we understand what he/she is teaching us.

yes no   12. We are afraid to tell the teacher when we do not understand something.

yes no   13. Our teacher usually punishes the whole class.

yes no   14. We wish our class could have the same teacher next year.

yes no   15. Our teacher grades fairly.

yes no   16. Our teacher is not friendly towards children.

yes no   17. Our teacher likes some children better than others.

yes no   18. When we do something wrong, our teacher is able to correct us without hurting our feelings.

yes no   19. We know what our teacher expects of us.

yes no   20. Our teacher is often too busy to help us when we need help.

NURSERY RHYMES
WITH A SYNONYM TWIST

(A dictionary and a thesaurus are helpful)

RATIONALE:
>This is an interesting lesson on using synonyms. The grade level provides the choice of synonyms used.

OBJECTIVE:
>Provided with nursery rhymes, each cooperative learning group will select a rhyme and then replace key words in the rhyme with synonyms.

MATERIALS:
>Each cooperative learning group will need paper and pencils. A dictionary and/or thesaurus for each group will be helpful. Each group will also need a copy, or one for each, of a nursery rhyme (included are five that work well).

PROCEDURE:
1. Allow the students to assemble into their cooperative learning groups.

2. For this reading skills project, they will select a recorder. If appropriate for the grade level, they may also select or take turns being the researcher who does the dictionary/thesaurus work.

3. Their selection, or your selection, of the nursery rhyme they will work with can innovatively be left up to you.

4. Forty-five minutes should be ample time for them to exchange the key words in the rhyme with a synonym.

FOLLOW-UP:
>When they have completed the project assignment, allow them a few minutes to practice reading it and then present it as a *choral* reading. Praise, appraise and support their ambitions. Other groups may critique. Display their creations.

An example of the project and five other nursery rhymes that work well:

Three Blind Mice

Three Visually Impaired Rodents
Three rodents with defective eyesight! Look how they scamper!
They all scamper toward the agriculturist's spouse,
She chopped off their appendage with a kitchen utensil.
Have you ever seen such a catastrophe in your existence
As three rodents with defective eyesight?

Tom, Tom, the Piper's Son

The Little Girl with a Curl

Wee Willie Winkie

Jack and Jill

The Cat and the Fiddle

CREATING A 'WHAT TECHNOLOGY IS' COLLAGE

RATIONALE:

This project will create an atmosphere that encourages all children to become aware of and interested in technological pursuits.

OBJECTIVE:

The students, in cooperative learning groups, will create a collage.

This project provides a stage, a jumping off point, for discussion of what technology is and what technologists do.

By including women and men, girls and boys, people of color, different nationalities, and people with disabilities, you will begin to show that technology is equitable for all.

MATERIALS:

You will need a large piece of display paper for each group. You will also, finally, be able to use that supply of magazines you have been saving all this time. The magazines should have ample pictures of technology at work. Glue, scissors, and magic markers will also be needed for each group of students.

PROCEDURE:

1. Students and desks are arranged for this activity.

2. Personnel are elected.

3. Discussion takes place: "What is technology?" and "What do technologists do?"

4. This is an excellent word to use in "Semantic Webbing." With the students' prior knowledge, they should be able to provide the who, what, why, when, and where of technology.

5. Supplies are dispensed and they can use the magic markers to list words on their collages from the webbing. They then can choose, cut, and paste pictures from the magazines to put on their paper.

FOLLOW-UP:
Display their creations, clean up the work area. Praise, appraise, compare, contrast, and support their ambitions.

HARE AND TORTOISE RACE

RATIONALE:

A fun activity. The students will race objects.

OBJECTIVE:

Two teams of students will use a tagboard tortoise and hare to have a race. The objects will race along a hand held string. The results will be posted on the board on a bar graph (mathematics project).

MATERIALS:

You will need to cut out an outline of a tortoise and hare on tagboard. They should be the same size and weight. Punch a hole at the top of each and attach a large paper clip into the hole. You will also need two 20 foot pieces of string or yarn.

PROCEDURE:

1. Divide the class into two teams (they can count off 1-2-1-2, etc.).

2. Move the desks to make an open area 20 feet by 6 feet.

3. Attach one end of each string to a permanent object. This object should be low to the floor.

4. Now, stretch the string out its entire length.

5. A member of each team can now take either the tortoise or hare, place the string through the clip attached to the top of the animal and by holding their arms up make the animal move down the string. They will soon experiment and observe ways to make the animal move faster.

6. Be prepared for some loud team spirited noise.

FOLLOW-UP:
As a mathematics graphing lesson, graph the results on a bar graph you have prepared on the board. This can also be a good rainy day activity.

PEA AND TOOTHPICK BUILDING

RATIONALE:

This construction play will increase skills by demanding dexterity, imagination and creativity.

OBJECTIVE:

The students, working in cooperative learning groups, will design and build an object.

Provided with toothpick rods and pea connectors, the groups of students will work as a team to construct some type of building or object. A 40 minute time period is sufficient. Flat patterns, domes, geometric forms, or the Sears Tower are all possible.

MATERIALS:

You will need one package of whole dried peas. You will need a "large" bowl in which to soak the peas (do this the day before and let soak until project time). You need to fill the bowl with water one inch over the level of the peas. You will also need one box of round toothpicks for each group and a small bowl to evenly divide the peas.

PROCEDURE:

1. The students will arrange the room for the group project.

2. They will elect the necessary group personnel.

3. Explain that the criteria demands that each group works on the same project from start to finish. They will use the toothpicks as rods and the peas as connectors. They will be given 40 minutes to build. Construction can be as simple or complex as they want.

FOLLOW-UP:

After the time limit, allow them to display their creations (if left to stand overnight the peas will dry making the object strong). Whole class discussion can reveal problems encountered and positive solutions taken. Appraise, praise, compare, contrast and support their ambitions.

Remember: a few peas go a long ways. One box of toothpicks is 250. As part of this project, as it's related to mathematics, give them a calculator and have them compute the total cost of their group's construction.

Peas = 1¢
Toothpicks = 5¢

PAPER MODEL AIRPLANE BUILDING AND FLYING

RATIONALE:

Each member of a group will manipulate paper in order to propel it a specified distance.

OBJECTIVE:

Each team member of the cooperative learning group will, within a 20 minute time period, change a piece of paper so that it can be propelled a distance of 10 feet.

PROCEDURE:

1. Allow the students to arrange the room for their groups.

2. For this project they will need only a supply person, everyone will be engineers.

    a. Each member of the group must be able to construct an object that can move through the air at least 10 feet.

    b. During the 30 minute time period they will be allowed to test their creation two times and then make any necessary changes.

c. They do not all have to build the same thing; members of a group may assist each other.

d. A final testing of all construction will be held at the end of the time limit.

4. They may begin as soon as they have their supplies. They **are not** told, but, they may construct their objects by folding or by crumpling. They may build a plane, a flying saucer, a ball, etc.

FOLLOW-UP:

After the time period, allow each student two chances to propel their object the specified distance.

Discussion time is held to talk about problems encountered and remedial strategies used.

PINWHEELS

RATIONALE:
> The students will discover and prove that air has movement. This project is a good science activity.

OBJECTIVE:
> With the aid of an electric fan and specified materials, students will discover and prove that air has movement.

MATERIALS:
> Supply each student with a new pencil that has an eraser. They will also need a straight pin and a square piece of paper at least 6 inches per side. You may also supply a prepared square with directions printed on it for making a pinwheel. Each group of students will need scissors. A small electric fan is also needed.

PROCEDURE:
> 1. The students can assemble into their groups and elect their supply personnel.
>
> 2. The criteria are listed on the board:
>
>   a. Each member of the group must construct some type of object to show that air moves.
>
>   b. They must use all three supplied materials.
>
>   c. They may or may not decide to follow the directions for the pinwheel if supplied to them.
>
>   d. They will be given 25 minutes of construction time.
>
>   e. They may test their object 2 times before the end of the time limit.
>
>   f. Each member is free to experiment and they may assist members of their own group.

FOLLOW-UP:

        After the time period allow each group to demonstrate their creations. Discussion time is held to talk about their accomplishments.

        Discuss problems encountered and remedial strategies used.

Cooperative Learning,
Thinking and Problem Solving

A POLAROID POLARITY

(Access to a Polaroid camera is necessary)

RATIONALE:

> The integration of visuals into the learning process. This activity stresses the importance of individual responsibility and the enhancement of self-esteem.

OBJECTIVE:

> Supplied with a Polaroid camera, only one is necessary, each cooperative learning group will have their group picture taken and then compose a biographical sketch of their group.

MATERIALS:

> Access to a Polaroid camera is necessary. If one is not available to you, then write to the company. They have a great education program for the classroom. The film is expensive, but you may budget for it and the company also offers incentives. Pencil and paper will also be needed.

PROCEDURE:

> 1. Have the students assemble into their cooperative learning groups. Remember, these groups do not have to be static. However, the

groups should work together five or six times before you change them.

2. You, the teacher, may now take each group's picture. Students may be allowed to do this too; they are able to handle the camera with minimum prior guidance.

3. After the picture is taken, allow each group to watch it develop. This happens very quickly. They should not yet handle it.

4. While the picture is "appearing" you can present the necessary criteria.

   a. They will be given 30-40 minutes to work with pencil and paper.

   b. Together, they will write a brief biographical sketch of each member of the group. Things that may be included are:

      • their names
      • their ages
      • the role they feel they have in the group
      • their feelings about the group

FOLLOW-UP:
At the completion of this activity they may share what they have written. You may also want to type what they have written and attach the picture to this biographical sketch. Discuss any problems they may have had. Praise their motivations and creativity.

Expansion across the curriculum

1. Take photos of your school and make a collage.

2. Take photos of common objects and write an advertisement.

3. Do you have some new construction at school? Work with your students on a time-line project.

4. Take photos of individuals and let them write an autobiography.

5. Search for an unusual object. Take a picture and let the students write a creative story.

6. Photograph people while they are working at school. The students will be surprised at all the varied careers necessary to operate the school. This may also spark self-interest in a career for them.

7. Take a photo to illustrate a point. Perhaps your playground is littered; the photo can show this to the students in the classroom. Go from there!

GRAHAM CRACKER DECORATING

RATIONALE:
The students, working in cooperative learning groups, will produce an edible product.

OBJECTIVE:
The groups of 5-6 students will, in 20-30 minutes' time, have decorate graham crackers with frosting and candies.

MATERIALS:
1 cellophane wrapped packet of graham crackers for each group, 1 tube of frosting in each group. A variety of flavored candies may also be dispensed in small dishes. 1-2 paper plates for each group and a napkin for each student is optional. Each group may also be given a frosting spreading device. Some sort of beverage may also be provided.

PROCEDURE:
1. Have the groups assemble into a small work group.

2. They should be able to decide by how what types of personnel they will need.

3. The objective for each group is to be given 20 minutes to decorate their crackers, and to put them into a display. Emphasis is on neatness and attractiveness in the display of the finished product.

4. Once the supply personnel has obtained the necessary materials, they may begin.

5. Again, remember to give them a few minutes warning before the time is used up.

GRAHAM CRACKER DECORATING

RATIONALE:

The students, working in cooperative learning groups, will produce an edible product.

OBJECTIVE:

The groups of 5-6 students will, in a 20 minute time frame, decorate graham crackers with frosting and candies.

MATERIALS:

1 cellophane wrapped packet of graham crackers for each group. 1 tube of frosting for each group. A variety of flavored candies may also be dispensed in cupcake liners. 2-3 paper plates for each group and a napkin for each student is advisable. Each group may also be issued a frosting spreading device. Some sort of beverage may also be provided.

PROCEDURE:

1. Have the groups assemble into their work areas.

2. They should be able to decide by now what types of personnel they will need.

3. The objective for each group is to be given 20 minutes to decorate their crackers, and to put them into a display. Emphasis is on neatness and attractiveness in the display of the finished product.

4. Once the supply personnel has obtained the necessary materials, they may begin.

5. Again, remember to give them a few minutes warning before the time is used up.

FOLLOW-UP:
Allow each group to show off their displayed product. Praise and support their efforts. Again, problems may result from the group dynamics or from the thinking, manipulation, or operation of the materials. Discuss problems encountered and positive solutions taken. Clean up the work area and allow them to enjoy the snack.

BUILD IT – MOVE IT

RATIONALE:

The cooperative learning groups will each devise a method of attaching three objects, that move simultaneously, to a stationary base.

OBJECTIVE:

Supplied with a 12" x 24" piece of cardboard or tagboard, each group will construct a base piece and then with selected materials, attach three pieces of the cardboard/tagboard in such a manner that these three pieces become interdependent for some type of movement.

MATERIALS:

Each group will need 1 - 12" x 24" piece of cardboard/tagboard. A pair of scissors heavy enough to cut the board, 6 tacks, 6 paperclips, 6 straight pins, 3 rubber bands, one piece of string 24 inches long, 1 ruler and a pencil.

PROCEDURE:

1. Students get into their cooperative learning groups.

2. They will elect their needed personnel (they will need a supply person and then they all become engineers).

3. Criteria can be discussed and/or listed on an overhead.

   a. First, the supply personnel will have to come to the supply table to obtain the cardboard/tagboard and other allotted supplies.

   b. Then each group will make a 12" x 12" base piece from this board.

   c. Next they will use the remaining cardboard/tagboard and cut it into three differently shaped pieces (the sizes and shapes are the group's choice). These pieces are then to be fastened to the base. The choice of materials used to fasten the three pieces to the base is left entirely up to each group.

   d. Movement is to be initiated by touching **one** piece. All three of the attached pieces are required to have movement and they must also be dependent on each other for movement (in other words, when one piece moves, the other two do too).

   e. They will be given 45 minutes to work.

FOLLOW-UP:

After each group has demonstrated their creation, discussion can take place. Discuss any problems they encountered and solutions used. Praise, appraise, compare, contrast, and support their ambitions. Creations are displayed and the room is brought back to order.

RED . . . YELLOW . . . BLUE
or
MAKE ME A RAINBOW

RATIONALE:

The students, working in cooperative learning groups, will discover and watch colors mix and change.

OBJECTIVE:

Supplied with a large sheet of paper and liquid tempera paint, each group will experiment with the mixing of red, yellow, and blue (the primary colors) to discover the myriad of colors possible.

MATERIALS:

White corrugated or rolled paper (approximately 3' x 6', one for each group). Liquid tempera paint (2 - 16 oz. containers of each color is sufficient). Small straws (one for each member of each group). Paper towels (this really is not a messy project).

PROCEDURE:

1. If each group is capable and time allows, have them measure and

cut the paper they will need (in this case, meter or yardstick and scissors will need to be made available).

2. Each group will need quite a large open area. If the students can lie down around this 3' x 6' piece of paper, it works best (school hallways work great).

3. They will each be given a straw. This is their artist tool and they will be blowing through it onto the paint.

4. After the students have stationed themselves around the paper, pour about an ounce of each of the three primary colors on the paper in front of each of them (a triangle arrangement works best).

5. They can now spend 20-30 minutes blowing this liquid paint all around the paper. What a wonderful rainbow of colors they will create!

6. After the fun, allow the creations to dry and display them as wall hangings. They are beautiful!

FOLLOW-UP:
Discussion may take place as to what they have learned and how much they enjoyed the project. Bring the room back to order.

45 MINUTES TO 4

RATIONALE:
The cooperative learning groups will each devise usable products out of pieces of paper.

OBJECTIVE:
Supplied with 4 sheets of varying grades and sizes of paper, each group of students, within 45 minutes, will devise 4 usable products that meet the criteria established.

MATERIALS:
Each group will need 4 sheets of paper; 2 - 12" x 18" construction, 1 - 9" x 12" construction and 1 - 8 1/2" x 11" plain, colors are your choice). 1 roll of cellophane or masking tape, scissors, a pencil and ruler are also needed.

PROCEDURE:
1. Students get into their cooperative learning groups.

2. For this project, they will need to select supply personnel. Later, he/she and the rest become engineers.

3. Criteria can be discussed or viewed on an overhead. From the supplied materials they are to construct 4 out of 5 of the listed objects.
   - one object that can hold water
   - one object that will keep rain off one member's head
   - a device that will magnify a voice
   - a stand-up name card to identify your cooperative learning group (they will enjoy naming their group)
   - a device that shows the exact measurement of one member's waist

4. They will have 45 minutes to finish the 4 constructions.

FOLLOW -UP:

Each group must be able to explain and demonstrate their creations (yes, the water container too). Discuss problems encountered and solutions taken. Praise, appraise, compare, contrast, and support their ambitions.

THE PAPER PLATE DILEMMA

(This project makes use of a calculator)

RATIONALE:

Help! Our Earth is being polluted with paper plates. We need to think of ways to use these clean used plates other than trashing them. Help!

OBJECTIVE:

Supplied with a specified number of paper plates for each member of the team and given 30 minutes to work, members will have to "buy" materials to help them devise different methods of recycling these clean used paper plates.

MATERIALS:

1 calculator, paper and a pencil for each group and one regular size paper plate for each member of the group. Additional clean used paper plates can be kept at the supply table for students' use. The following listed items are offered at a cost to each group.

- 1 block of clay = $1.00
- 1 roll of masking or cellophane tape = $1.00
- 1 large straw = $.10 or 1 small straw = $.05
- 1 large box of crayons = $.90

- scissors = $.50 a pair
- paper clips = $.05 each
- straight pins or map pins = $.01 each
- yarn = $.05 an inch
- paper punch = $.50

PROCEDURE:
1. Students get into their cooperative learning groups.
2. The group's personnel is discussed and selected. They will need a supply person, a cost analyst and engineers.
3. They are supplied with a calculator, 1 piece of paper, a pencil, and a paper plate for each member.
4. Now they are told that the earth is becoming polluted with paper plates and it's against the law to dispose of them. They are to work, as a team, to devise other uses for these clean used plates.

5. They may combine the plates, use them singly, and/or use additional plates from the supply table.

6. They may purchase items to help them experiment and create. They will be "charged" a price for each item they purchase and they **must** calculate the cost of their project. They should strive for economy.

7. Each item they create must be different in some way.

8. All pieces should be used. We do not want to create more waste than we are recycling. They will be charged $.10 for each wasted product, including additional plates.

9. They may be given 45 minutes to work.

FOLLOW-UP:
Each group must be able to explain their creations and costs involved in making them. Praise, appraise, compare, contrast, and support their ambitions. Discuss problems encountered and solutions taken. Display the products and bring the room back to order.

NOTE: If you feel that your students may have problems coming up with ideas in the time allotted, then you may do this; at the beginning of the week, explain to the class what this week's project will be. Then begin listing **their** useful suggestions for items on the board. By Friday you should have a good list and they can pick and choose from it. Use and change the project to fit your particular needs.

Some items they may come up with are: flowers, pictures, dishes, clocks, pinwheels, funnels, vases, storage containers, frisbees, slippers, potholders, mailboxes, hanging containers, flying saucers, various holiday bonnets.

You may want to substitute various size plastic milk containers for the paper plates. Items may include: ballcatcher, toilet brush holder, planter, feed scoop, sandbox toy, Chinese lanterns, funnel, piggy-bank, sailboat, bird feeder, vase, pencil holder, catch-all, shop/work-room organizer.

MARSHMALLOW OLYMPICS

RATIONALE:
> The cooperative learning groups will work together to efficiently move an object.

OBJECTIVE:
> Supplied with a marshmallow, each group will use a variety of objects to move a marshmallow through an obstacle course as efficiently as possible.

MATERIALS:
> One large marshmallow for each group (the remainder of the bag may be used as prizes). Each group will also need 1 teaspoon, 1 straw, 1 toothpick, 1 kleenex tissue, a pencil, 12 inches of string, 1 piece of 6" x 6" paper, 1 ruler, and a can with the top off.

PROCEDURE:
> 1. The students will assemble into their cooperative learning groups. Personnel is discussed and selected (they need only a supply person and then they all become engineers).
>
> 2. Now, given time to think, each member of the group is to choose an item that will help only them move the marshmallow.
>
> 3. Each time the marshmallow is moved, it must be moved by a different member. If there are not enough members, then some students may have two turns.
>
> 4. For each obstacle they are successful at they will receive two free marshmallows. If they drop the marshmallow, that movement is unsuccessful.
>
> 5. The marshmallow itself **must never** be touched by hand.
>
> 6. They will have 20 minutes.

7. The movements for the marshmallow are these:
   - from the supply depot to your work area
   - into a can
   - out of the can onto their work area
   - over a 12 inch space
   - from desktop to floor
   - from floor to desktop
   - delivered back to the supply depot

FOLLOW-UP:
Praise their imaginations and efforts. Award them the earned marshmallows for obstacles successfully coursed. Discuss problems encountered and solutions taken. Bring the room back to order.

A NEWSPAPER ACTIVITY

(Scavenger Hunt)

RATIONALE:
Newspaper exploration.

OBJECTIVE:
Provided with a newspaper, each cooperative learning group will locate and select pictures and/or articles to complete a "Scavenger Hunt" list.

MATERIALS:
The list of required pictures and/or articles to find. A full-size newspaper for each group (many small town newspapers have the best variety of pictures). A large sheet of paper on which to display the pictures and articles. Scissors, glue, pencil, and calculator.

PROCEDURE:
1. Students assemble into their cooperative learning groups.

2. Discuss what personnel they need. For this project they may want to select an editor. They will also need supply personnel, researchers and layout designers (cutters and pasters).

3. The list of things to find is distributed to each group. All have the same list.

4. Criteria is explained:

   a. They will be given 45 minutes to work.

   b. Each team is to try to locate, in their newspaper, each item on the list.

   c. They will select the items, cut them out, and paste them onto the display sheet.

   d. They should label their items.

Cooperative Learning, Thinking and Problem Solving

e. They will be given 5 points for each item they complete.

f. If they cannot find an item in their own newspaper, they may negotiate and purchase it from another group by paying that group 5 points per item.

FOLLOW-UP:

At the end of the time limit, assess each group to see what items they were successful at locating. Calculate the points accumulated. Distribute recognition (prizes, rewards, trophies, etc.). Discuss problems encountered and solutions taken. Praise their ambitions.

EXTENSION:

The following list can be altered and revised to fit various grade levels and/or classroom objectives in Social Studies, Science, Language Arts, etc.

Scavenger Hunt List

1. A picture of a person wearing glasses.
2. A picture of a map.
3. A number larger than 50.
4. A picture with both women and men in it.
5. A picture of something to travel in.
6. A picture of something to eat.
7. The name of a town, other than where you live.
8. A picture of an athlete.
9. A picture of an animal.
10. A picture of a building.

Add these for grade three

11. An advertisement for a toy.
12. A weather report.
13. A picture of an important government figure.
14. A picture of a movie or TV star.
15. The name of a newspaper.

Add these for grade four

16. A picture of someone from a foreign country.
17. Any sort of puzzle.
18. A classified ad for a job.
19. An article or advertisement for a concert.
20. A cartoon.

FOOD GROUPS COLLAGE

(Dairy, Grain, Meat/Protein, Fruit/Vegetable)

RATIONALE:
Awareness of food nutrition.

OBJECTIVE:
Each cooperative learning group will be given 40 minutes to select pictures, to make a collage, that depicts the one food group they are working with. Emphasis for this project may be on the layout and display of the design.

MATERIALS:
Three or four magazines for each group. A large **square** box (approximately 24" x 24" per side). A sheet of paper for the display for each group (it should be the size of the sides of the box). Scissors, magic markers, and glue. You will also need four pieces of paper with each piece having one of the food groups printed on it. For higher grades, if you want to add dimension to the work, you may use thin sheets of styrofoam cut to necessary shapes and fasten them between some pictures and the display paper. This will make them "stand out."

PROCEDURE:
1. Students assemble into their cooperative learning groups.

2. Discuss what personnel they will need. For this project they will need supply personnel, nutritionist researchers, and layout designers (cutters and pasters).

3. Devise a method allowing groups to select the food group they will work with.

4. The objective is explained:

    a. They have 40 minutes to work.

    b. They are to select pictures that depict their food group and then attach them to the display paper.

    c. Emphasis may be on design and display.

5. Each finished product will be attached to one side of the square box.

6. The "display box" can have a placecard attached at the top labeling the display.

7. Supply personnel may now obtain the materials their group needs. The time limit begins.

FOLLOW-UP:

Display the cooperative creation for all to see. Assess the success of the project. Praise their ambitions.

EXTENSION:

Each group may also plan a "Luncheon Special" menu. A blank copy of a menu is included. Each group may decorate the menu, as well as plan the menu.

_____ Restaurant

Luncheon Special

Milk Group _____

Meat Group _____

Fruit-Vegetable Group _____

Grain Group _____

Our Luncheon Special is shown below.

SPELLING WITH OUR FINGERS

(A good mid-year project)

RATIONALE:
Students will fingerspell sentences using the American Sign Language Manual Alphabet.

OBJECTIVE:
The cooperative learning groups will be given the Manual Alphabet to study for 30 minutes. After the study time, 15 minutes will be used for groups to perform their sentences. Each group will spell two out of three provided sentences.

MATERIALS:
One copy per student of the provided Manual Alphabet. One copy per group of the suggested three sentences.

PROCEDURE:
1. Students assemble into their cooperative learning groups.

2. Groups will need to select a supply person to pick up necessary materials from the central dispersal area.

3. The criteria is explained:

   a. They have 30 minutes to study the Manual Alphabet and to practice their words/sentences.

   b. They must collectively choose two of the three sentences they wish to fingerspell.

   c. Each member will fingerspell one or two words per sentence depending upon the size of the group and the length of the sentence. These choices are left entirely up to the groups.

d. As words are fingerspelled, they should be voiced. The proper procedure to follow is to pronounce the word as a whole as you fingerspell it. Lower grades may find it necessary to voice each letter as the word is spelled.

e. An extended criteria could be to hand out a copy of the Manual Alphabet to each student early in the week and have them practice at their leisure. Then, when groups are displaying their cooperative sentences, have the remaining groups try to read the sentences; instead of the fingerspeller voicing his/her word as they fingerspell it.

4. Supply personnel may now collect the needed materials. The time limit begins.

FOLLOW-UP:
The groups will have 15 minutes to cooperatively display their sentences in front of the other groups. Discuss problems encountered. Praise their ambitions.

EXTENSION:
Depending upon the grade level, you may choose to have each group compose their own sentences. They may also be required to guess (read) what each group has fingerspelled.

(American Sign Language Manual Alphabet is found on page 69.)

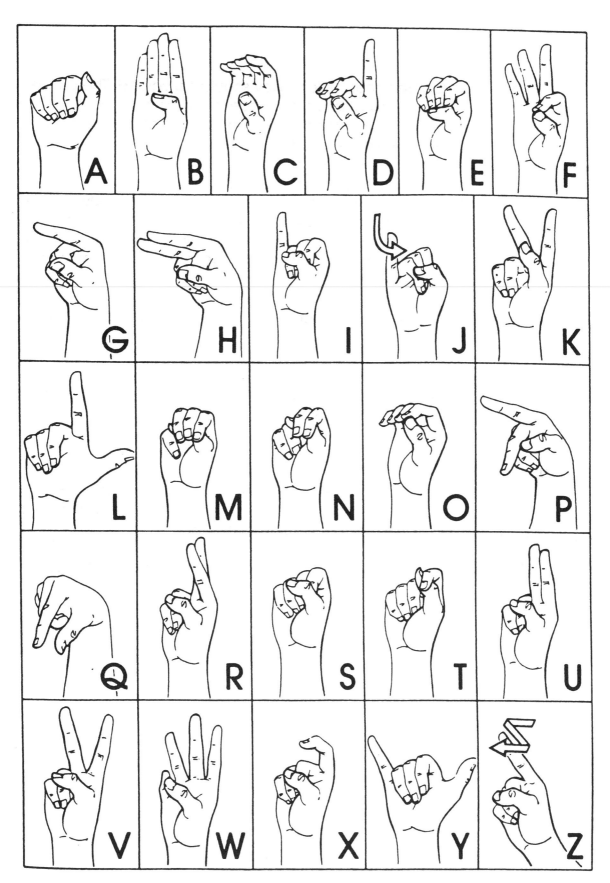

Tom Humphries, Carol Padden, Terrence J. O'Rourke, "The Manual Alphabet", in *A Basic Course in American Sign Language*, Silver Spring, MD: T.J. Publishers, Inc., 1980), p. 235

Spelling With Our Fingers
suggested sentences

----

1. My bus comes at seven.

2. They have a dog named Jack.

3. It is very cold at my house.

----

1. Two plus three is five.

2. Last night we ate pizza for supper.

3. My sister is six years old.

----

1. We want to eat hotdogs.

2. The sun feels very warm today.

3. We like to go to the zoo.

----

1. Math class is very fun.

2. The frog jumped over the log.

3. My coat is nice and warm.

----

1. Quit running in the hall.

2. Our dad drives a big truck.

3. We want to go to the lake.

Cooperative Learning,
Thinking and Problem Solving

DESERT SURVIVAL

RATIONALE:
How to survive in the Sahara Desert.

OBJECTIVE:
Each cooperative learning group will, within a 30-40 minute time frame, have to make a decision of staying with a downed airplane in a desert, or walking to civilization. If the choice is to walk, then each group will have to choose items (7 out of 20), to take with them to help survive. They must also give a reason for choosing each item.

MATERIALS:
A list of 20 items in their survival box for each group. A pencil and piece of paper for each group to write their reasons for choosing the 7 out of 20 items.

SCENARIO: (To be explained to the groups.)
They are on an airplane that is forced down in the Sahara Desert in North Africa. The plane is off course, was traveling at 200 miles per hour and lost radio contact 5 hours ago. All passengers are okay. There is no guarantee of a rescue, nor of continued survival. They know it is a 3 day journey north, to a city. What should they do?

PROCEDURE:
1. Students assemble into their cooperative learning groups.

2. Groups will need to select a supply person to pick up the necessary materials from the central dispersal area.

3. The scene has been set. The criteria is explained:

    a. They will have from 30-40 minutes to work.

    b. First, they must decide if they will stay with the airplane or walk, North, to civilization. **Everyone** in their group **must** be in agreement to stay or go.

c. If as a group they have decided to walk, they must choose items to take with them. Only 7 of the 20 items can be chosen to help them survive the desert trek.

d. If they have decided to stay with the airplane, they must give the rationale as to their collective decision.

e. Each group must write why the seven items were chosen, or why they decided to stay.

4. Supply personnel may now collect the needed materials. The time limit begins.

FOLLOW-UP:

A lively discussion ensues. What was each groups' choice, to stay or to walk? Were there any difficulties in debating the decision? If the unanimous choice was to walk, which seven items were chosen, and why? Relate to them that if they had chosen to stay with the downed airplane, they will probably be found soon and survive. If they had chosen to walk to civilization, they probably will not survive. (They will, of course, think differently, and that is fine.) Discuss problems encountered. Praise their ambitions. Console those who perished!!!

NOTE:

Don't be afraid of this one. Second graders did very will with the project.

Cooperative Learning,
Thinking and Problem Solving

Desert Survival Box

a hand mirror

a parachute

a pencil

1 book of matches

2 cans of Coke

scissors

an electric fan

1 tube of toothpaste

a 10 dollar bill

1 school Math book

a long sleeve jacket

an umbrella

a safety pin

T.V. Guide

nail clippers

a compass

a portable radio

1 jar of spinach

a hunting bow and 1 arrow

1 box of saltine crackers

Teacher's Notes . . .

Teacher's Notes . . .

Teacher's Notes . . .

Teacher's Notes . . .

Teacher's Notes . . .

Teacher's Notes . . .

Teacher's Notes . . .